Confession

Advice and encouragement from Pope Benedict XVI

Compiled by
Fr Donncha Ó hAodha

*All booklets are published thanks to the
generous support of the members of the
Catholic Truth Society*

CATHOLIC TRUTH SOCIETY
PUBLISHERS TO THE HOLY SEE

Contents

The source of purification and holiness

Benedict XVI repeatedly invites us to "rediscover" the Sacrament of Confession as the powerful source of purification and holiness which it truly is. In his characteristically encouraging style, the Holy Father presents the Sacrament of Reconciliation to all the faithful as a treasure to be loved and cherished ever anew. This sacrament of healing brings the hope and joy we all so deeply need.

Because the Lord pardons us and deepens our identification with him in Confession, this sacrament is a prerequisite for the profound renewal of the Church. In fact the power of this Sacrament to build up the Church is evident in different ways all the time. One thinks of happy families nurtured by regular reception of the sacrament of pardon, and of many young people who commit themselves to Christ and discover their vocation in the Church also through recourse to this source of forgiveness and grace. A spectacular public witness to the vivifying role of Confession is of course the World Youth Day experience. One thinks for example of the hundreds of confessionals in the park of "El Retiro" in the centre of Madrid at World Youth Day 2011, where Benedict XVI also spent time administering this sacrament. Confession is the sacrament of eternal youthfulness.

Benedict XVI's teaching on this sacrament is in total continuity with that of his Blessed predecessor. From the very start of his pontificate Bl. John Paul II emphasised the vital importance of the Sacrament of Confession.[1] His second encyclical, *Dives in Misericordia* (30 November 1980) is a profound meditation on God's fatherly mercy, while his post-synodal Apostolic Exhortation *Reconciliatio et Paenitentia* (2 December 1984) is a deep and comprehensive teaching regarding "Reconciliation and Penance in the Mission of the Church today" which has lost nothing of its timeliness. Bl. John Paul II addressed the subject of sacramental Penance again and again throughout the 27 years of his pontificate. In his Apostolic Letter, *Novo Millenio Ineunte* (6 January 2001) at the close of the Great Jubilee of the Year 2000, the Pope placed the Sacrament of Reconciliation[2] among "certain pastoral priorities"[3] for the Church in her "starting afresh from Christ".[4] The publication in 2002 of the Apostolic Letter in the form of *motu proprio*, *Misericordia Dei* "on certain aspects of the celebration of the Sacrament of Penance," was another earnest appeal "to undertake a vigorous revitalization of the Sacrament of Reconciliation."[5] By his example and teaching, and also by his institution of the second Sunday of Easter (or *"Dominica in albis"*) as "Divine Mercy Sunday",[6] Bl. John Paul II constantly proclaimed Christ as Redeemer, who through his Cross, has become divine Mercy for us.

Rediscover the mystery of mercy

Benedict XVI is echoing Bl. John Paul II in issuing a call to rediscover Christ as the *sacramentum pietatis* (mystery of mercy). This call is addressed to all the faithful; to laity and priests alike, to those who regularly go to Confession and to those who have been away for a long time. To "rediscover" Confession is to seek once again "to comprehend … what is the breadth and length and height and depth, and to know the love of Christ which surpasses knowledge" (*Eph* 3:18-19). St Josemaría Escrivá, whom Benedict XVI mentions among "the great saints of the past" who gave an example of "faithful and generous availability … to hear confessions,"[7] wrote in *The Way* (n. 309): "What depths of mercy there are in God's justice! For, in the judgements of men, he who confesses his fault is punished; and in the judgement of God, he is pardoned. Blessed be the holy Sacrament of Penance!"

Our great danger is to underestimate God's love for each of us. To appreciate Confession ever anew is to rediscover our Lord's tender determination for our holiness and abiding happiness. This in turn can spur us on to deeper conversion and greater commitment to holiness in our daily lives. The "encounter with God who makes himself infinite mercy for us"[8] not only cleanses us but also strengthens us to be apostles of joy for our friends and neighbours, and for all humanity. We cannot receive the grace of Confession without becoming witnesses to hope among others, notwithstanding our own limitations and defects. Significant in this regard is the statement from the Holy See that the Year of Faith "provides an appropriate occasion in which all can approach the Sacrament of Penance with greater faith, and more frequently."[9]

Communicate the joy of forgiveness

Pope Benedict XVI sets Confession within the perspective of spreading the Gospel. Indeed, as he points out, the forgiveness of sins *is* the Good News. The Sacrament of Penance is a service to the well-being of all humanity and the entire world, since there is no true peace or justice unless sin is overcome. The faithful become sources of hope and joy when they themselves have received forgiveness and peace from the Lord. Those who receive divine forgiveness must communicate their joy all around them.

Like St Peter after the miraculous catch of fish, we might feel unworthy of such a mission. Conscious of our own sinfulness, we could be tempted to shy away from speaking about sin and Reconciliation. Like St Peter we might be inclined to ask the Lord to look elsewhere for better ambassadors: "Depart from me, for I am a sinful man, O Lord" (*Lk* 5:8). But like St Peter, we too hear the

divine reassurance: "Do not be afraid; henceforth you will
be catching men" (*Lk* 5:10). What counts is to place our
trust in the Lord, to seek to be his instruments, and like St
Peter, to begin time and again in our efforts to be faithful:
"Lord, you know everything; you know that I love you"
(*Jn* 20:17).

Pope Benedict XVI's teaching on Confession provides
us with a valuable formation for the New Evangelization
to which the entire Church is called at this time. By helping
us deepen in our knowledge of this wonderful sacrament,
the Holy Father seeks to help all "to grasp and rightly
understand in what font they have been washed, by whose
Spirit they have been reborn, by whose Blood they have
been redeemed".[10]

The following text is composed of questions any of us
might care to ask about this sacrament. The answers all
come from various instances of the Holy Father's teaching.

The Sacrament of Confession

How would you describe the Sacrament of Confession?

The Sacrament of Confession [is] a true encounter with God's love, which every person needs in order to live in joy and peace.[11]

The Sacrament of Penance is one of the Church's precious treasures, since authentic world renewal is accomplished only through forgiveness. Nothing can improve the world if evil is not overcome.[12]

The Sacrament of Reconciliation … in the deepest sense of the word is a sacrament of healing. The real wound in the soul, in fact, the reason for all our other injuries, is sin. And only if forgiveness exists, by virtue of God's power, by virtue of Christ's love, can we be healed, can we be redeemed.[13]

God's holiness is not merely an incandescent power before which we are obliged to withdraw, terrified. It is a power of love and therefore a purifying and healing power. God descends and becomes a slave, he washes our feet so that we may come to his table. In this, the entire mystery of Jesus Christ is expressed. In this, what redemption means becomes visible. The basin in which he washes us is his love, ready to face death. Only love has that purifying power which washes the grime from us and elevates us to God's heights. The basin that purifies us is God himself, who gives himself to us without reserve - to the very depths of his suffering and his death. He is ceaselessly this love that cleanses us; in the sacraments of purification - Baptism and the Sacrament of Penance - he is continually on his knees at our feet and carries out for us the service of a slave, the service of purification, making us capable of God. His love is inexhaustible, it truly goes to the very end.[14]

What takes place in this Sacrament … is especially a mystery of love, a work of the merciful love of the Lord.

"God is love" (*1 Jn* 4:16): in this simple affirmation the Evangelist John has enclosed the revelation of the entire mystery of the Triune God. And in meeting with Nicodemus, Jesus, foretelling his passion and death on the Cross, affirms: "For God so loved the world that he gave his only Son, that whoever believes in him should not perish but have eternal life" (*Jn* 3:16).

We all need to draw from the inexhaustible fountain of divine love, which is totally manifested to us in the mystery of the Cross, in order to find authentic peace with God, with ourselves and with our neighbour. Only from this spiritual source is it possible to draw the indispensable interior energy to overcome the evil and sin in the ceaseless battle that marks our earthly pilgrimage toward the heavenly homeland.[15]

What are the biblical roots of this sacrament?

"Those who are well have no need of a physician, but those who are sick; I came not to call the righteous, but sinners" (*Mk* 2:17). The good news of the Gospel consists precisely in this: offering God's grace to the sinner![16]

Indeed, mercy is the central nucleus of the Gospel message; it is the very name of God, the Face with which he revealed himself in the Old Covenant and fully in Jesus Christ, the incarnation of creative and redemptive Love. May this merciful love also shine on the face of the Church and show itself through the sacraments, in particular that of Reconciliation, and in works of charity, both communitarian and individual. May all that the Church says and does manifest the mercy God feels for man, and therefore for us.[17]

The New Testament speaks on every page of God's love and mercy, which are made visible in Christ. Jesus, in fact, who "receives sinners and eats with them" (*Lk* 15:2), and with authority affirms: "Man, your sins are forgiven you".

Which Gospel passages can help to understand Confession?

We read that Jesus "healed many who were sick with various diseases, and cast out many demons" (*Mk* 1:34); in another passage from St Matthew it says that Jesus "went about all Galilee, teaching in their synagogues and preaching the Gospel of the Kingdom and healing every disease and every infirmity among the people" (*Mt* 4:23). Jesus leaves no room for doubt: God whose Face he himself revealed is the God of life, who frees us from every evil. The signs of his power of love are the healings he performed. He thus shows that the Kingdom of God is close at hand by restoring men and women to their full spiritual and physical integrity. I maintain that these cures are signs: they are not complete in themselves but guide us towards Christ's message, they guide us towards God and make us understand that man's truest and deepest illness is the absence of God, who is the source of truth and love.[18]

While Jesus was preaching, among the many sick people who were brought to him there was a paralytic on a stretcher. On seeing him the Lord said: "My son, your sins are forgiven" (*Mk* 2:5). And since some of those present were scandalized at hearing these words, he added: "That you may know that the Son of man has authority to forgive sins on earth', he said to the paralytic, "I say to you, rise, pick up your mat, and go home'" (*Mk* 2:10-11). And the paralytic went away healed. This Gospel account shows that Jesus has the power not only to heal a sick body but also to forgive sins; indeed, the physical recovery is a sign of the spiritual healing that his forgiveness produces. Sin is effectively a sort of paralysis of the spirit from which only the power of God's merciful love can set us free, allowing us to rise again and continue on the path of goodness.[19]

Jesus said to the leper: "Be made clean!" According

to the ancient Jewish law (cf. *Lv* 13-14), leprosy was not only considered a disease but also the most serious form of ritual "impurity". It was the priests' duty to diagnose it and to declare unclean the sick person who had to be isolated from the community and live outside the populated area until his eventual and well-certified recovery. Thus, leprosy constituted a kind of religious and civil death, and its healing a kind of resurrection. It is possible to see leprosy as a symbol of sin, which is the true impurity of heart that can distance us from God. It is not in fact the physical disease of leprosy that separates us from God as the ancient norms supposed but sin, spiritual and moral evil. This is why the Psalmist exclaims: "Blessed is he whose fault is taken away, / whose sin is covered", and then says, addressing God: "I acknowledged my sin to you, / my guilt I covered not. / I said, 'I confess my faults to the Lord' / and you took away the guilt of my sin" (32[31]: 1, 5) …This miracle thus has a strong symbolic value. Jesus, as Isaiah had prophesied, is the Servant of the Lord who "has borne our griefs / and carried our sorrows" (*Is* 53:4). In his Passion he will become as a leper, made impure by our sins, separated from God: he will do all this out of love, to obtain for us reconciliation, forgiveness and salvation.[20]

Jesus healed 10 people sick with leprosy, a disease in those times considered a "contagious impurity" that required ritual cleansing (cf. *Lv* 14:1-37). Indeed, the "leprosy" that truly disfigures the human being and society is sin; it is pride and selfishness that spawn indifference, hatred and violence in the human soul. No one, save God who is Love, can heal this leprosy of the spirit which scars the face of humanity. By opening his heart to God, the person who converts is inwardly healed from evil.[21]

Would you cite any Gospel in particular?

The Evangelist St Luke pays special attention to the theme of Jesus' mercy. In fact, in his narration we find some episodes that highlight the merciful love of God and of Christ, who said that he had come to call, not the just, but sinners (cf. *Lk* 5:32). Among Luke's typical accounts there is that of the conversion of Zacchaeus ... Zacchaeus is a publican, indeed, he is the head of the publicans of Jericho, an important city on the River Jordan. The publicans were the tax collectors who collected the tribute that the Jews had to pay to the Roman Emperor, and already for this reason they were considered public sinners. What is more, they often took advantage of their position to extort money from the people. Because of this Zacchaeus was very rich but despised by his fellow citizens. So when Jesus was passing through Jericho and stopped at the house of Zacchaeus, he caused a general scandal. The Lord, however, knew exactly what he was doing. He wanted, so to speak, to gamble, and he won the bet: Zacchaeus, deeply moved by Jesus' visit, decided to change his life, and promised to restore four times what he had stolen. "Today salvation has come to this house", Jesus says, and concludes: "The Son of Man came to seek and to save the lost" … Zacchaeus welcomed Jesus and he converted because Jesus first welcomed him! He did not condemn him but he met his desire for salvation.[22]

In … chapter 15 of St Luke Jesus recounts the three "parables of mercy". When he speaks of "the shepherd who goes after the lost sheep, of the woman who looks for the lost coin, of the father who goes to meet and embrace his prodigal son, these are no mere words: they constitute an explanation of his very being and activity" (Encyclical *Deus Caritas Est,* n. 12). In fact, the shepherd who finds the stray sheep is the Lord himself who lays upon his shoulders, with the Cross, sinful humanity, in order to redeem it. The prodigal son, then, in the third parable, is a young man who having obtained his inheritance from his father "took his journey into a far country, and there, he squandered his property in loose living" (*Lk* 15:13). Reduced to a penniless state he was obliged to work as a servant, even accepting to satisfy his hunger with food intended for animals. Then, the Gospel says, "He came to himself" (*Lk* 15:17). "The speech he prepares for his homecoming reveals to us the full extent of the inner pilgrimage he is now making... leading "home"... to himself and to the father". (Benedict XVI *Jesus of Nazareth, Doubleday,* 2007, Chapter 7, p. 205). "I will arise and go to my father, and I will say to him, "Father, I have sinned against Heaven and before you; I am no longer worthy to be called your son; treat me as one of your hired servants'" (*Lk* 15:18-19). St Augustine wrote: "The Word himself calls you to return, and with him is a place of unperturbed rest, where love is not forsaken unless it first forsakes. "While he was yet at a distance, his father saw him and had compassion, and ran and embraced him and kissed him" (*Lk* 15:20) and, full of joy, had a feast prepared.[23]

It is necessary today to assist those who confess to experience that divine tenderness to repentant sinners which many Gospel episodes portray with tones of deep feeling. Let us take, for example, the passage in Luke's Gospel that presents the woman who was a sinner and was forgiven (cf. *Lk* 7:36-50). Simon, a Pharisee and a rich dignitary of the town, was holding a banquet at his home in honour of Jesus. In accordance with a custom of that time, the meal was eaten with the doors left open, for in this way the fame and prestige of the homeowner was increased. All at once, an uninvited and unexpected guest entered from the back of the room: a well-known prostitute. One can understand the embarrassment of those present, which did not seem, however, to bother the woman. She came forward and somewhat furtively stopped at Jesus' feet. She had heard his words of pardon and hope for all, even prostitutes; she was moved and stayed where she was in silence. She bathed Jesus' feet with tears, wiped them dry with her hair, kissed them and anointed them with fragrant ointment. By so doing, the sinner woman wanted to express her love for and gratitude to the Lord with gestures that were familiar to her, although they were censured by society.

Amid the general embarrassment, it was Jesus himself who saved the situation: "Simon, I have something to say to you". "What is it, Teacher?", the master of the house asked him. We all know Jesus' answer with a parable which we can sum up in the following words which the Lord addressed basically to Simon: "You see? This woman knows she is a sinner; yet prompted by love, she is asking for understanding and forgiveness. You, on the other hand, presume yourself to be righteous and are perhaps convinced that you have nothing serious for which to be forgiven".

The message that shines out from this Gospel passage is eloquent: God forgives all to those who love much. Those who trust in themselves and in their own merits are, as it were, blinded by their ego and their heart is hardened in sin. Those, on the other hand, who recognize that they are weak and sinful entrust themselves to God and obtain from him grace and forgiveness. It is precisely this message that must be transmitted.[24]

When did our Lord institute this Sacrament?

The Risen Christ instituted it at the very moment he gave the disciples his peace and his Spirit … Jesus breathed on the Apostles and said: "Receive the Holy Spirit. If you forgive the sins of any, they are forgiven; if you retain the sins of any, they are retained" (*Jn* 20:22-23).[25]

The Holy Spirit who creates faith within us at the moment of our Baptism enables us to live as children of God, aware and consenting, in accordance with the image of the Only-Begotten Son. The power to forgive sins is also a gift of the Holy Spirit.[26]

The visit of the Risen One is not limited to the space of the Upper Room but goes beyond it, to the point that all can receive the gift of peace and life with the "creative Breath". In fact Jesus said twice to his disciples, "Peace be with you". And he added, "As the Father has sent me, even so I send you". Having said this he breathed on them, saying "Receive the Holy Spirit. If you forgive the sins of any, they are forgiven; if you retain the sins of any, they are retained". This is the mission of the Church, eternally assisted by the Paraclete: to bear the Good News, the joyful reality of God's merciful love, in order, as St John says, "that you may believe that Jesus is the Christ, the Son of God, and that believing you may have life in his name" (20:31).[27]

Who forgives sins in Confession?

Indeed, God is not an inexorable sovereign who condemns the guilty but a loving father whom we must love, not for fear of punishment, but for his kindness, quick to forgive.[28]

Christ, the true Son of God, who became a true man, took all our sins upon himself. He himself is the point of contact between human wretchedness and divine mercy. In his heart the grievous mass of the evil perpetrated by humanity is dissolved and life is renewed.[29]

Jesus can grant forgiveness and the power to forgive because he himself suffered the consequences of sin and dispelled them in the flame of his love. Forgiveness comes from the Cross; he transforms the world with the love that is offered. His heart opened on the Cross is the door through which the grace of forgiveness enters into the world. And this grace alone is able to transform the world and build peace.[30]

Jesus, coming from the Father, visited peoples' homes on our earth and found a humanity that was sick, sick with fever, the fever of ideologies, idolatry, forgetfulness of God. The Lord gives us his hand, lifts us up and heals us. And he does so in all ages; he takes us by the hand with his Word, thereby dispelling the fog of ideologies and forms of idolatry. He takes us by the hand in the sacraments, he heals us from the fever of our passions and sins through absolution in the Sacrament of Reconciliation.[31]

Who, therefore, saves the world and man? The only answer we can give is: Jesus of Nazareth, Lord and Christ, Crucified and Risen. And where is the Mystery of the death and Resurrection of Christ that brings about salvation? In Christ's action through the Church, and in particular in the sacrament of the Eucharist, which makes the redemptive sacrificial offering of the Son of God present, in the sacrament of Reconciliation in which from the death of sin one returns to new life, and in every other sacramental act of sanctification (cf. *Presbyterorum Ordinis,* n. 5). It is therefore important to encourage an appropriate catechesis to help the faithful understand the value of the sacraments.[32]

The Spirit of Jesus Christ is the power of forgiveness. He is the power of Divine Mercy. He makes it possible to start all over again - ever anew. The friendship of Jesus Christ is the friendship of the One who makes us people who forgive, the One who also forgives us, raises us ceaselessly from our weakness and in this very way educates us, instils in us an awareness of the inner duty of love, of the duty to respond with our faithfulness to his trust.[33]

What is the relationship between Penance and the Eucharist?

The faithful ... must seek to receive and to venerate the Most Holy Sacrament with piety and devotion, eager to welcome the Lord Jesus with faith, and having recourse, whenever necessary, to the sacrament of reconciliation so as to purify the soul from every grave sin.[34]

The banquet of the Eucharist is an anticipation of the final feast in Heaven, to which the Lord invites us every day and in which we must take part, clothed in the wedding garment of his grace. Should it happen that we soil or even tear this garment with sin, God's goodness does not reject or abandon us to our destiny but rather offers us, with the Sacrament of Reconciliation, the possibility of restoring the wedding garment to the pristine state required for the feast.[35]

I would … like to invite pastors and the faithful to take a renewed interest in their preparation for receiving the Eucharist. Despite our weakness and sin, Christ wants to make his dwelling place in us. This is why we must do everything in our power to receive him with a pure heart, continuously rediscovering through the Sacrament of forgiveness that purity which sin has stained, "that [our] minds be attuned to [our] voices" (cf. *Sacrosanctum Concilium,* n. 11), according to the Council's invitation. Sin in fact, especially serious sin, impedes the action of Eucharistic grace within us. Moreover, those who cannot receive Communion because of their situation will find a saving power and effectiveness in a Communion of desire and from participation at the Eucharist.[36]

Through your love for the Eucharist you will also rediscover the Sacrament of Reconciliation, in which the merciful goodness of God always allows us to make a fresh start in our lives.[37]

The centre of [St John Mary Vianney's] entire life was the Eucharist, which he celebrated and adored with devotion and respect. Another fundamental characteristic of this extraordinary priestly figure was his diligent ministry of confession. He recognized in the practice of the sacrament of penance the logical and natural fulfilment of the priestly apostolate, in obedience to Christ's mandate: "if you forgive the sins of any, they are forgiven; if you retain the sins of any, they are retained" (cf. Jn 20: 23). St John Mary Vianney thus distinguished himself as an excellent, tireless confessor and spiritual director. Passing "with a single inner impulse from the altar to the confessional", where he spent a large part of the day, he did his utmost with preaching and persuasive advice to help his parishioners rediscover the meaning and beauty of the sacrament of Penance, presenting it as an inherent demand of the Eucharistic presence (cf. *Letter to Priests for the inauguration of the Year for Priests*).[38]

Why is there a special need to promote this Sacrament today?

Because of the dramatic events of our time, the theme of mutual forgiveness is felt with increased urgency, yet there is little perception of our fundamental need of God's forgiveness, of our justification by him. Our modern consciousness – and in some way all of us are "modern" - is generally no longer aware of the fact that we stand as debtors before God and that sin is a reality which can be overcome only by God's initiative. Behind this weakening of the theme of justification and of the forgiveness of sins is ultimately a weakening of our relation with God. In this sense, our first task will perhaps be to rediscover in a new way the living God present in our lives, in our time and in our society.[39]

John Paul II said: "He who lets himself be filled with this love can no longer deny his guilt. The 'loss of the sense of sin' derives in the last analysis from 'the more radical and hidden loss of the sense of God'" (*Homily, Inauguration of the San Lorenzo International Centre,* 13 March 1983, n. 5).[40]

In our time, humanity needs a strong proclamation and witness of God's mercy. Beloved John Paul II, a great apostle of Divine Mercy, prophetically intuited this urgent pastoral need. He dedicated his Second Encyclical to it and throughout his Pontificate made himself a missionary of God's love to all peoples.

After the tragic events of 11 September 2001, which darkened the dawn of the third millennium, he invited Christians and people of good will to believe that God's Mercy is stronger than all evil, and that only in the Cross of Christ is the world's salvation found.[41]

We live in a cultural context marked by the hedonistic and relativistic mindset that tends to delete God from the horizon of life and does not encourage the acquisition of a clear set of values to refer to that would help one to discern good from evil and develop a proper sense of sin.

This situation makes even more urgent the service of stewards of Divine Mercy. We must not forget, in fact, that a sort of vicious circle exists between the clouding of the experience of God and the loss of the sense of sin. However, if we look at the cultural context in which St John Mary Vianney lived we see that in various aspects it was not so very unlike our own. In his time too, in fact, there was a mentality hostile to faith, expressed by forces that even sought to prevent the exercise of the ministry. In this circumstance, the Holy Curé d'Ars "chose the Church as his home", in order to lead people to God.[42]

Of course, sacramental Reconciliation is one of the moments in which personal freedom and an awareness of self need to be expressed particularly clearly. It is perhaps also for this reason, in an epoch of relativism and of the consequent attenuated awareness of one's being, that this sacramental practice is also weakened.

Examination of conscience has an important pedagogical value. It teaches us how to look squarely at our life, to compare it with the truth of the Gospel and to evaluate it with parameters that are not only human but are also borrowed from divine Revelation. Comparison with the Commandments, with the Beatitudes and, especially, with the Precept of love, constitutes the first great "school of penance".

In our time, marked by noise, distraction and loneliness, the penitent's conversation with the confessor can be one of the few - if not the only - opportunities to be truly heard in depth.[43]

The contemporary world continues to present contradictions so clearly outlined by the Fathers of the Second Vatican Council (cf. *Gaudium et Spes*, nn. 4-10): we see a humanity that would like to be self-sufficient, where more than a few consider it almost possible to do without God in order to live well; and yet how many seem sadly condemned to face the dramatic situations of an empty existence, how much violence there still is on the earth, how much solitude weighs on the soul of the humanity of the communications era![44]

These days, the correct formation of believers' consciences is without a doubt one of the pastoral priorities because, unfortunately, as I have reaffirmed on other occasions, to the extent that the sense of sin is lost, feelings of guilt increase which people seek to eliminate by recourse to inadequate palliative remedies. The many invaluable spiritual and pastoral tools that contribute to the formation of consciences should be increasingly developed.[45]

In a word, it seems that today there is even loss of the "sense of sin", but in compensation the "guilt complex" has increased.

Who can free the heart of humankind from this yoke of death if not the One who by dying overcame for ever the power of evil with the omnipotence of divine love?

As St Paul reminded the Christians of Ephesus: "God, who is rich in mercy, out of the great love with which he loved us, even when we were dead through our trespasses, made us alive together with Christ" (*Eph* 2:4).[46]

Why do you encourage us to "rediscover" sacramental Confession?

In the Sacrament of Confession we can always start out afresh in life. He welcomes us, he restores to us our dignity as his children. Let us therefore rediscover this sacrament of forgiveness that makes joy well up in a heart reborn to true life.[47]

[God] "is gracious and merciful, slow to anger, rich in kindness and relenting in punishment" (*Jl* 2:13). Joel's invitation, addressed to his listeners, also applies to us. Let us not hesitate to rediscover the friendship of God lost by sin; encountering the Lord, we experience the joy of his forgiveness.[48]

Through the surpassing power of Christ's grace, entrusted to frail human ministers, the Church is constantly reborn and each of us is given the hope of a new beginning. Let us trust in the Spirit's power to inspire conversion, to heal every wound, to overcome every division, and to inspire new life and freedom. How much we need these gifts! And how close at hand they are, particularly in the sacrament of Penance! The liberating power of this sacrament, in which our honest confession of sin is met by God's merciful word of pardon and peace, needs to be rediscovered and reappropriated by every Catholic. To a great extent, the renewal of the Church ... throughout the world depends on the renewal of the practice of Penance and the growth in holiness which that sacrament both inspires and accomplishes.[49]

The Sacrament of Reconciliation (...) asks to be reassessed as a fundamental means for spiritual growth and for facing today's challenges with strength and courage.[50]

Let us invoke the Virgin Mary whom God preserved from every stain of sin so that she may help us to avoid sin and to have frequent recourse to the Sacrament of Confession, the sacrament of forgiveness, whose value and importance for our Christian life must be rediscovered today.[51]

What do the Saints say about Confession?

Initially [St Augustine] thought that once he was baptized, in the life of communion with Christ, in the sacraments, in the Eucharistic celebration, he would attain the life proposed in the Sermon on the Mount: the perfection bestowed by Baptism and reconfirmed in the Eucharist. During the last part of his life he understood that what he had concluded at the beginning about the Sermon on the Mount - that is, now that we are Christians, we live this ideal permanently - was mistaken. Only Christ himself truly and completely accomplishes the Sermon on the Mount. We always need to be washed by Christ, who washes our feet, and be renewed by him. We need permanent conversion. Until the end we need this humility that recognizes that we are sinners journeying along, until the Lord gives us his hand definitively and introduces us into eternal life. It was in this final attitude of humility, lived day after day, that Augustine died.

This attitude of profound humility before the only Lord Jesus led him also to experience an intellectual humility. Augustine, in fact, who is one of the great figures in the history of thought, in the last years of his life wanted to submit all his numerous works to a clear, critical examination. This was the origin of the *Retractationum* ("Revision"), which placed his truly great theological thought within the humble and holy faith that he simply refers to by the name *Catholic,* that is, of the Church. He wrote in this truly original book: "I understood that only One is truly perfect, and that the words of the Sermon on the Mount are completely realized in only One - in Jesus Christ himself. The whole Church, instead - all of us, including the Apostles -, must pray everyday: Forgive us our sins as we forgive those who sin against us" (*De Sermone Domini in Monte,* I, 19, 1-3).[52]

In the *Exposition of the Gospel according to Luke*, [St Ambrose] … expressed his wonder at the gifts that God added to his forgiveness: "You see how good God is and ready to pardon sins: not only does he give back everything he had taken away, but he also grants unhoped for gifts". Zechariah, John the Baptist's father, lost the ability to speak because he did not believe the angel, but subsequently, in pardoning him, God granted him the gift of prophecy in the hymn of the Benedictus: "The one who could not speak now prophesies", St Ambrose said, adding that "it is one of the greatest graces of the Lord, that those who have denied him should confess belief in him. Therefore, no one should lose trust, no one should despair of the divine reward, even if previous sins cause him remorse. God can change his opinion if you can make amends for your sin" (2, 33: *SAEMO, XI,* Milan-Rome, 1978, p. 175).[53]

[St. Antonio de Sant'Ana Galvao] was greatly sought out as a confessor, because he was zealous, wise and prudent. It is characteristic of those who truly love that they do not want the Beloved to be offended; the conversion of sinners was therefore the great passion of our saint. Sister Helena Maria, the first religious sister destined to belong to the *Recolhimento de Nossa Senhora da Conceição*, witnessed to what Frei Galvão had said to her: "*Pray that the Lord our God will raise sinners with his mighty arm from the wretched depths of the sins in which they find themselves.*" May this insightful admonition serve as a stimulus to us to recognize in the Divine Mercy the path towards reconciliation with God and our neighbour, for the peace of our consciences.[54]

What about Our Lady and this Sacrament?

The mystery of the Immaculate Conception is a source of inner light, hope and comfort. Amidst the trials of life and, especially, the contradictions that man experiences within and around himself, Mary, Mother of Christ, tells us that Grace is greater than sin, that God's mercy is more powerful than evil and it is able to transform it into good. Unfortunately, every day we experience evil, which is manifested in many ways including relationships and events, but whose root is in the human heart, a wounded, sick heart that is incapable of healing itself. Sacred Scripture reveals to us that the origin of all evil is disobedience to God's will and that death has the upper hand because human freedom has yielded to the temptation of the Evil One.[55]

"Repent, and believe in the Gospel" (*Mk* 1:15). Jesus began his public life with this invitation that continues to resonate in the Church to the point that in her apparitions, the Virgin Most Holy has renewed this appeal, especially in recent times … Let us think in particular of Fatima, where … from 13 May to 13 October 1917, the Virgin appeared to the three little shepherd children: Lucia, Jacinta and

Francisco.[56] The Virgin Mary, Queen of Peace, shared until
his martyrdom her Son Jesus' fight with the Devil and
continues to share in it to the end of time. Let us invoke
her motherly intercession so that she may help us always
to be witnesses of Christ's peace and never to sink so low
as to make compromises with evil.[57]

Let us pray to Mary Most Holy, who accompanies
and sustains us … so that she may help every Christian
to rediscover the greatness, I would say, the beauty,
of conversion.

May she help us understand that doing penance and
correcting one's conduct is not simply moralism, but the most
effective way to change oneself and society for the better.

An adage expresses it well: to light a candle is worth
more than to curse the darkness.[58]

I ask the Virgin Mary, Mother of Mercy, to sustain the
ministry of priest confessors and to help every Christian
community to understand ever more the value and
importance of the Sacrament of Penance for the spiritual
growth of every one of the faithful.[59]

Going to Confession

Why go to Confession?

Only reconciliation with God can give us true healing, true life, because a life without love and without truth would not be life.[60]

Only God's love can change man's life and thus every society from within, for it is God's infinite love alone that sets him free from sin, which is the root of all evil. If it is true that God is justice, we should not forget that above all he is love. If he hates sin, it is because he loves every human person infinitely. He loves each one of us and his fidelity is so deep that it does not allow him to feel discouraged even by our rejection.[61]

To be converted means (…) for each one of us, to believe that Jesus "has given himself for me", dying on the Cross (cf. *Ga* 2:20) and, risen, lives with me and in me. Entrusting myself to the power of his forgiveness, letting myself be taken by his hand, I can come out of the quicksands of pride and sin, of deceit and sadness, of selfishness and of every false security, to know and live the richness of his love.[62]

The bathing that purifies us once and for all and must not be repeated is Baptism - being immersed in the death and Resurrection of Christ, a fact that profoundly changes our life, giving us as it were a new identity that lasts, if we do not reject it as Judas did. However, even in the permanence of this new identity, given by Baptism, for convivial communion with Jesus we need the "washing of the feet". What does this involve? It seems to me that the *First Letter of St John* gives us the key to understanding it. In it we read: "If we say we have no sin, we deceive ourselves, and the truth is not in us. If we confess our sins, he is faithful and just, and will forgive our sins and cleanse us from all unrighteousness" (1:8ff.). We are in need of the "washing of the feet", the cleansing of our daily sins, and for this reason we need to confess our sins as St John spoke of in this Letter. We have to recognize that we sin, even in our new identity as baptized persons. We need confession in the form it has taken in the Sacrament of Reconciliation. In it the Lord washes our dirty feet ever anew and we can be seated at table with him.[63]

Why should sin be taken seriously?

It is precisely the closure of ourselves to the Lord and the failure to take the path of our own conversion that lead to death, to the death of the soul.[64]

What the Bible calls "iniquity" that is, sin ... fundamentally consists in disobeying God, which means a lack of love as the origin of every material and social injustice.[65]

The true enemy to be feared and fought is sin, the spiritual evil, which at times unfortunately, afflicts even the members of the Church. We live in the world, the Lord says, but we are not of the world (cf. *Jn* 17:10,14), and we must beware of its seduction. But we must fear sin, and for this we must be strongly rooted in God, in solidarity for the good, in love, in service. It is what the Church and her ministers, together with the faithful, have done and continue doing with fervent commitment for the spiritual and material good of people in every part of the world.[66]

There exists a deep solidarity among all the members of the Body of Christ. It is not possible to love Christ without loving his brothers and sisters. For their salvation John Mary Vianney decided to become a priest: "to win souls for the good God", as he said when, at eighteen years of age, he announced his vocation, just as Paul had said: "to win as many as I could" (*1 Co* 9:19). The Vicar General had told him: "there is not much love of God in the parish; you will bring it there". In his priestly passion, this holy parish priest was merciful like Jesus in meeting each sinner. He preferred to insist on the attractive aspect of virtue, on God's mercy, in comparison to which our sins are like "grains of sand". He pointed to the merciful love of God which had been offended. He feared that priests would become "insensitive" and accustomed to the indifference of their faithful: "Woe to the Pastor – he would warn – who remains silent while God is offended and souls are lost".[67]

What are the effects of going to Confession?

In the Sacrament of Penance, the Crucified and Risen Christ purifies us through his ministers with his infinite mercy, restores us to communion with the heavenly Father and with our brothers and makes us a gift of his love, his joy and his peace.[68]

You will experience "the forgiveness of sins; reconciliation with the Church; recovery, if it has been lost, of the state of grace; remission of the eternal punishment merited by mortal sins, and remission, at least in part, of the temporal punishment which is the consequence of sin; peace, serenity of conscience and spiritual consolation; and an increase of spiritual strength for the struggle of Christian living" for every day (*Compendium of the Catechism of the Catholic Church*, n. 310). With the penitential cleansing of this Sacrament, we are readmitted to full communion with God and the Church, a trustworthy companion because she is the "universal sacrament of salvation" (*Lumen Gentium*, n. 48).[69]

The forgiveness which Christ gives to us in the Sacrament of Penance is a source of interior and exterior peace and makes us apostles of peace in a world where divisions, suffering and the tragedies of injustice, hatred and violence and the inability to be reconciled to one another in order to start again with a sincere pardon, unfortunately continue.[70]

Why confess to a priest rather than directly to God?

Sin is not only a "personal", individual thing between myself and God. Sin always has a social dimension, a horizontal one. With my personal sin, even if perhaps no one knows it, I have damaged the communion of the Church; I have sullied humanity. And therefore this social, horizontal dimension of sin requires that it be absolved also at the level of the human community, of the community of the Church, almost physically.

Thus, this second dimension of sin, which is not only against God but concerns the community too, demands the Sacrament, and the Sacrament is the great gift in which through confession, we can free ourselves from this thing and we can really receive forgiveness of a full readmission to the community of the living Church, of the Body of Christ. And so, in this sense, the necessary absolution by the priest, the Sacrament, is not an imposition – let us say – on the limits of God's goodness, but, on the contrary, it is an expression of the goodness of God because it shows me also concretely, in the communion of the Church, I have received pardon and can start anew … The absolution of the priest, sacramental absolution, is necessary to really absolve me of this link with evil and to fully reintegrate me into the will of God, into the vision of God, into his Church and to give me sacramental, almost bodily, certitude: God forgives me, he receives me into the community of his children. I think that we must learn how to understand the Sacrament of Penance in this sense: as a possibility of finding again, almost physically, the goodness of the Lord, the certainty of reconciliation.[71]

God wants only goodness and life for us; he provides for the health of our soul through his ministers, delivering us from evil with the Sacrament of Reconciliation, so that no one may be lost but all may have the opportunity to convert.[72]

With Baptism you are already born to new life in virtue of God's grace. Nonetheless, since this new life has not eliminated either the weakness of human nature or the inclination to sin, we are given the opportunity to receive the Sacrament of Confession. Every time that you do so with faith and devotion, after an attentive examination of conscience, God's love and mercy open your heart to Christ's minister. To him, and thereby to Christ himself, you express your sorrow for the sins you have committed with the firm determination to sin no more in the future and the readiness to accept joyfully the acts of penance to which he will direct you, to make reparation for the damage caused by the sin.[73]

Moreover the integral confession of sins teaches the penitent humility, recognition of his or her own frailty and, at the same time, an awareness of the need for God's forgiveness and the trust that divine Grace can transform his life. Likewise, listening to the confessor's recommendations and advice is important for judging actions, for the spiritual journey and for the inner healing of the penitent.

Let us not forget how many conversions and how many truly holy lives began in a confessional! The acceptance of the penance and listening to the words "I absolve you from your sins", are, lastly, a true school of love and hope that guides the person to full trust in the God Love, revealed in Jesus Christ, to responsibility and to the commitment to continuous conversion.[74]

The sins that we commit distance us from God and, if we do not humbly confess them, trusting in divine mercy, they will finally bring about the death of the soul.[75]

St Ambrose ... often recalled the reasons that motivated him to invoke pardon from God.

"We have a good Lord who wants to forgive everyone", he recalled in his *Treatise on Penance,* and he added: "If you want to be justified, confess your fault: a humble confession of sins untangles the knot of faults... You see with what hope of forgiveness you are impelled to make your confession" (2, 6, 40-41: *Sancti Ambrosii Episcopi Mediolanensis Opera [SAEMO],* XVII, Milan-Rome, 1982, p. 253).[76]

How often should one go to Confession?

In our Christian life we must always aspire to conversion and ... when we receive the Sacrament of Reconciliation frequently the desire for Gospel perfection is kept alive in believers. If this constant desire is absent, the celebration of the Sacrament unfortunately risks becoming something formal that has no effect on the fabric of daily life. If, moreover, even when one is motivated by the desire to follow Jesus one does not go regularly to confession, one risks gradually slowing his or her spiritual pace to the point of increasingly weakening and ultimately perhaps even exhausting it … The regular celebration of the Sacrament of Penance and a Christian life that aspires to holiness are inseparable elements of the same spiritual process for every baptized person.[77]

[An] … important element of the World Youth Days is the sacrament of Confession, which is increasingly coming to be seen as an integral part of the experience. Here we recognize that we need forgiveness over and over again, and that forgiveness brings responsibility. Openness to love is present in man, implanted in him by the Creator, together with the capacity to respond to God in faith. But also present, in consequence of man's sinful history (Church teaching speaks of original sin) is the tendency that is opposed to love – the tendency towards selfishness, towards becoming closed in on oneself, in fact towards evil. Again and again my soul is tarnished by this downward gravitational pull that is present within me. Therefore we need the humility that constantly asks God for forgiveness, that seeks purification and awakens in us the counterforce, the positive force of the Creator, to draw us upwards.[78]

I call on children and young people …to remain faithful to the Word of God and to the doctrine learnt, and also to assiduously approach Confession and the Eucharist, conscious of having been chosen and constituted to witness to the Truth.[79]

How does this Sacrament help towards holiness?

Paul and Barnabas, disagreed at the beginning of the second missionary journey because Barnabas was determined to take with them as a companion John called Mark, whereas Paul was against it, since the young man had deserted them during their previous journey (cf. *Ac* 13:13;15:36-40).

Hence there are also disputes, disagreements and controversies among saints. And I find this very comforting, because we see that the saints have not "fallen from Heaven". They are people like us, who also have complicated problems.

Holiness does not consist in never having erred or sinned. Holiness increases the capacity for conversion, for repentance, for willingness to start again and, especially, for reconciliation and forgiveness.

So it was that Paul, who had been somewhat harsh and bitter with regard to Mark, in the end found himself with him once again. In St Paul's last Letters, to Philemon and in his Second Letter to Timothy, Mark actually appears as one of his "fellow workers".

Consequently, it is not the fact that we have never erred but our capacity for reconciliation and forgiveness which makes us saints. And we can all learn this way of holiness.[80]

It must be a commitment of pastors and especially of confessors to highlight the close connection that exists between the Sacrament of Reconciliation and a life oriented decisively to conversion. It is necessary that between the practice of the Sacrament of Confession and a life in which a person strives to follow Christ sincerely, a sort of continuous "virtuous circle" be established in which the grace of the Sacrament may sustain and nourish the commitment to be a faithful disciple of the Lord.[81]

What is the point in going to Confession repeatedly to confess the same things?

It is very helpful to confess with a certain regularity. It is true: our sins are always the same, but we clean our homes, our rooms, at least once a week, even if the dirt is always the same; in order to live in cleanliness, in order to start again. Otherwise, the dirt might not be seen but it builds up. Something similar can be said about the soul, for me myself: if I never go to confession, my soul is neglected and in the end I am always pleased with myself and no longer understand that I must always work hard to improve, that I must make progress. And this cleansing of the soul which Jesus gives us in the Sacrament of Confession helps us to make our consciences more alert, more open, and hence, it also helps us to mature spiritually and as human persons … It is very helpful to confess regularly in order to foster the cleanliness and beauty of the soul and to mature day by day in life.[82]

The sacrament of Penance is important. It teaches me to see myself as God sees me, and it forces me to be honest with myself. It leads me to humility. The Curé of Ars once said: "You think it makes no sense to be absolved today, because you know that tomorrow you will commit the same sins over again. Yet," he continues, "God instantly forgets tomorrow's sins in order to give you his grace today." Even when we have to struggle continually with the same failings, it is important to resist the coarsening of our souls and the indifference which would simply accept that this is the way we are. It is important to keep pressing forward, without scrupulosity, in the grateful awareness that God forgives us ever anew - yet also without the indifference that might lead us to abandon altogether the struggle for holiness and self-improvement. Moreover, by letting myself be forgiven, I learn to forgive others. In recognizing my own weakness, I grow more tolerant and understanding of the failings of my neighbour.[83]

Does God not get tired of forgiving us?

God loves us in a way that we might call "obstinate" and enfolds us in his inexhaustible tenderness.[84]

"The Lord, the Lord, a merciful and gracious God, slow to anger, abounding in steadfast love and faithfulness"

(*Ex* 34:6). This is the Face of God. This self-definition of God expresses his merciful love: a love that triumphs over sin, covers it, eliminates it. We can always be sure of this goodness which does not abandon us. There can be no clearer revelation. We have a God who refuses to destroy sinners and wants to show his love in an even more profound and surprising way to sinners themselves, in order to always offer them the possibility of conversion and forgiveness.[85]

What about those who feel they are beyond forgiveness?

God excludes no one, neither the poor nor the rich. God does not let himself be conditioned by our human prejudices, but sees in everyone a soul to save and is especially attracted to those who are judged as lost and who think themselves so. Jesus Christ, the Incarnation of God, has demonstrated this immense mercy, which takes nothing away from the gravity of sin, but aims always at saving the sinner, at offering him the possibility of redemption, of starting again from the beginning, of converting.[86]

The errors we commit, even if they are serious, do not corrode the fidelity of his love.[87]

How is it possible not to open our hearts to the certainty that in spite of being sinners we are loved by God? He never tires of coming to meet us, he is always the first to set out on the path that separates us from him. The Book of Exodus shows us how Moses, with confident and daring pleas, succeeded, so to speak, in moving God from the throne of judgement to the throne of mercy (cf. 32:7-11). Penitence is the measure of faith and through it one returns to the Truth. The Apostle Paul writes: "I received mercy because I had acted ignorantly in unbelief" (*1 Tm* 1:13). [In] the parable of the son who goes "home", we note that when the elder brother appears, indignant at the festive welcome given to his brother, it is again the father who reaches out to him and begs him: "Son, you are always with me, and all that is mine is yours" (*Lk* 15:31). Only the faith can transform selfishness into joy and renew true relationships with our neighbour and with God. "It was fitting to make merry and be glad, for this your brother was dead, and is alive; he was lost, and is found" (*Lk* 15:32).[88]

How should one prepare for Confession?

Let us … prepare ourselves with a sincere examination of conscience to present ourselves to those to whom Christ has entrusted the ministry of Reconciliation. Let us confess our sins with contrite hearts, seriously determined to repeat them no more, and above all resolving to always stay on the road of conversion. We will thus experience true joy: the joy that derives from God's mercy, which is poured out in our hearts and reconciles us with him. This joy is contagious! *"You will receive power when the Holy Spirit has come upon you … and you will be my witnesses"* (*Ac* 1:8). Make yourselves heralds of this joy that comes from accepting the gifts of the Holy Spirit, bearing witness in your lives to the fruit of the Spirit: *"love, joy, peace, patience, kindness, goodness, faithfulness, gentleness, self-control"*; this is how St Paul lists the fruits of the Holy Spirit in his Letter to the Galatians (*Ga* 5:22) ...

Being Christian is the encounter with an event, a Person, which gives life a new horizon and with it a decisive direction (cf. *Deus Caritas Est*, n.1). Precisely in order to encourage this encounter, you are preparing to open your hearts to God, confessing your sins and receiving pardon and peace through the action of the Holy Spirit and by means of the Church's ministry. In this way room is made within us for the presence of the Holy Spirit, the third Person of the Most Holy Trinity who is the "soul", the "vital breath" of Christian life: the Spirit enables us "to grow... in an understanding of Jesus that becomes ever deeper and more joyful and at the same time to put the Gospel into practice" (*Message, 23rd World Youth Day*, n. 1) ...

Look at the Cross at this moment and let us welcome God's love, which is given to us from the Cross by the Holy Spirit who comes from the pierced side of the Lord...

O divine Heart of Jesus, from which Blood and Water flowed as a source of mercy for us, we trust in you. Amen![89]

What about spiritual guidance?

It is important also to have "travelling companions" on the journey of our Christian life. I am thinking of a Spiritual

Director, a Confessor, of people with whom it is possible to share one's own faith experience.[90]

I would like to say that the invitation to have recourse to a good spiritual father who can guide every individual to profound knowledge of himself and lead him to union with the Lord so that his life may be in ever closer conformity with the Gospel still applies for all priests, consecrated and lay people, and especially youth. To go towards the Lord we always need a guide, a dialogue. We cannot do it with our thoughts alone. And this is also the meaning of the ecclesiality of our faith, of finding this guide.[91]

"Spiritual direction" also contributes to forming consciences. Today there is a greater need than in the past for wise and holy "spiritual teachers": an important ecclesial service. This of course requires an inner vitality which must be implored as a gift from the Holy Spirit in intense and prolonged prayer and with a special training that must be acquired with care.[92]

Everyone, in fact, especially those who have heeded the divine call to follow Christ closely, needs to be accompanied personally by a guide reliable in doctrine and expert in the things of God, this guide can help people to watch out for facile forms of subjectivism, making available their own knowledge and experience lived in the following of Jesus.

It is a matter of establishing the same personal relationship that the Lord had with his disciples, the special bond with which he led them, following behind him, to embrace the Father's will (cf. *Lk* 22:42), namely, to embrace the Cross.[93]

Can you encourage us to renew our commitment to this Sacrament?

When I was Archbishop of Munich and Freising, in a meditation on Pentecost, I was inspired by a film entitled *Seelenwanderung* (Metempsychosis) to explain the Holy Spirit's action in a soul. The film tells of two poor friends who, because of their goodness, do not manage to make any headway in life. One day one of them had an idea: since he had nothing else to put on sale he would sell his soul. His soul is purchased cheap and enclosed in a box. From that time on, to his great surprise, everything changes in his life. He begins a rapid ascent, becomes richer, obtains great honours and by the time of his death is a consul very well endowed with money and possessions. From the moment when he freed himself of his soul he no longer had any concern or humanity. He had acted unscrupulously, caring only for profit and success. Man no longer mattered in the least. He himself no longer had a soul. The film, I concluded, shows impressively how the facade of success often conceals an empty life.

Apparently, the man had lost nothing, but he lacked a soul and with it lacked everything. It is obvious, I continued in that meditation, that the human being cannot literally dispose of his own soul since it is his soul that makes him a person. He remained, in fact, a human person, yet he had the frightful possibility of being inhuman, of remaining a person while at the same time selling and losing his own humanity. There is an immense gap between the human person and the inhuman being, yet it cannot be demonstrated; it is the truly essential thing, yet it is apparently unimportant (cf. *Suchen, was droben ist. Meditationen das Jahr hindurch,* LEV, 1985).[94]

The episode of the disciples of Emmaus (cf. *Lk* 24:13-35) [is] an account that never ceases to astonish and move us. This episode shows the effects that the Risen Jesus works in two disciples: conversion from despair to hope; conversion from sorrow to joy; and also conversion to community life. Sometimes, when we speak of conversion we think solely of its demanding aspect of detachment and renunciation. Christian conversion, on the contrary, is also and above all about joy, hope and love. It is always the work of the Risen Christ, the Lord of life who has obtained this grace for us through his Passion and communicates it to us by virtue of his Resurrection.[95]

In receiving the Sacrament of Confession, you will be able to experience the "gratuitous gift that God makes to us of his own life infused by the Holy Spirit into our soul to heal it of sin and to sanctify it" (*Catechism of the Catholic Church,* n. 1999), so that, united to Christ, we may become new creatures (cf. *2 Co* 5:17-18).[96]

We are told that whoever believes will have eternal life (cf. *Jn* 3:36). In faith, in this "transformation" that repentance brings, in this conversion, in this new way of living, we arrive at life, at real life.[97]

Conversion consists in freely and lovingly accepting to depend in all things on God, our true Creator, to depend on love. This is not dependence but freedom.

To be converted thus means not pursuing one's own personal success - that is something ephemeral - but giving up all human security, treading in the Lord's footsteps with simplicity and trust so that Jesus may become for each one, as Blessed Teresa of Calcutta liked to say, "my All in all".[98]

Let us allow ourselves to be healed by Jesus, who can and wants to give us God's light! Let us confess our blindness, our shortsightedness, and especially what the Bible calls the "great transgression" (cf. *Ps* 19[18]:13): pride. May Mary Most Holy, who by conceiving Christ in the flesh gave the world the true light, help us to do this.[99]

The Sacrament of Confession and Evangelization

How could we all promote this Sacrament?

What counts most is to make people understand that in the Sacrament of Reconciliation, whatever the sin committed, if it is humbly recognized and the person involved turns with trust to the priest-confessor, he or she never fails to experience the soothing joy of God's forgiveness.[100]

What about this Sacrament and vocations?

Always remember that you are a "temple of the Spirit"; let him dwell within you and docilely obey his promptings in order to make your contribution to building the Church (cf. *1 Co* 12:7) and to discern to what kind of vocation the Lord is calling you. Today, the world needs priests, consecrated men and women and Christian married couples. To respond to your vocation through one of these ways, be generous, help yourselves by having recourse to the Sacrament of Confession and the practice of spiritual direction on your journey as consistent Christians. Seek in particular to sincerely open your heart to the Lord Jesus, to offer him your unconditional "yes".[101]

Not only must the scarcity of ordinations to the priesthood in certain countries not discourage us, but it must also be an incentive to increase the number of places of silence and listening to the word, to better attend to spiritual direction and the sacrament of Confession. In this way God's voice, which always continues to call and to strengthen, may be heard and promptly followed by numerous young people.[102]

How does the Sacrament of Reconciliation help to spread the Gospel?

The Church carries out her service to Christ's peace above all in the ordinary presence and action among men and women, with the preaching of the Gospel and the signs of love and mercy that accompany it (cf. *Mk* 16:20).

Of course, among these signs it is mainly the Sacrament of Reconciliation that should be emphasized ... How important and, unfortunately, insufficiently understood is the gift of Reconciliation which sets hearts at rest! Christ's peace is only spread through the renewed hearts of reconciled men and women who have made themselves servants of justice, ready to spread peace in the world with the force of the truth alone, without descending to compromises with the world's mentality because the world cannot give Christ's peace: this is how the Church can be the leaven of that reconciliation which comes from God. She can only be so if she remains docile to the Spirit and bears witness to the Gospel, only if she carries the

Cross like Jesus and with Jesus. The saints of every epoch witness precisely to this![103]

Almighty and Merciful God. A Roman prayer, connected with the text of the Book of Wisdom, says: "O God, show your omnipotence through pardon and mercy". The summit of God's power is mercy, pardon. In our modern-day worldly concept of power, we think of someone who owns large estates, who has some say in the world of economics, who has capital and can influence the world of the market. We think of someone who has military power, who can threaten. Stalin's question, "How many armed divisions does the Pope have?" still characterizes the common idea of power. Whoever has power and many worldly effects may be dangerous, as he could threaten and destroy. But Revelations tells us. "It is not so"; true power is the power of grace and of mercy. In his mercy, God demonstrates true power.[104]

The Lord has power to forgive sins, and … nothing stands in the way of his mercy when we seek him with pure and contrite hearts! Let us never hesitate to ask his pardon especially through the Sacrament of Reconciliation so that we may become better instruments of his love for others.[105]

Let us pray to the Virgin Mary, perfect model of communion with Jesus, to be renewed by his love, so that we too may experience the joy of being visited by the Son of God, of being renewed by his love and of transmitting his mercy to others.[106]

How does this Sacrament benefit wider society and contribute to peace in the world?

Without the healing of souls, without the healing of man from within there can be no salvation for humanity.[107]

If we are to be true forces of unity, let us be the first to seek inner reconciliation through penance. Let us forgive the wrongs we have suffered and put aside all anger and contention. Let us be the first to demonstrate the humility and purity of heart which are required to approach the splendor of God's truth. In fidelity to the deposit of faith entrusted to the Apostles (cf. *1 Tm* 6:20), let us be joyful witnesses of the transforming power of the Gospel![108]

Endnotes

[1] Cf. Bl. John Paul II's first encyclical *Redemptor Hominis*, 4 March 1979, n. 20

[2] Cf. Bl. John Paul II, Apostolic Letter, *Novo Millenio Ineunte*, 6 January 2001, n. 37.

[3] Bl. John Paul II, Apostolic Letter, *Novo Millenio Ineunte*, 6 January 2001, n. 29.

[4] Cf. Bl. John Paul II, Apostolic Letter, *Novo Millenio Ineunte*, 6 January 2001, Chapter III.

[5] Bl. John Paul II, Apostolic Letter in the form of *motu proprio*, *Misericordia Dei*, 7 April 2002.

[6] Cf. Bl. John Paul II, *Homily at the Cononization of Sr Mary Faustina Kawolska*, 30 April 2000, n. 4.

[7] Benedict XVI, Address, 25 March 2011.

[8] Benedict XVI, Audience, 30 June 2010.

[9] Congregation for the Doctrine of the Faith, *Note with Pastoral Recommendations for the "Year of Faith"*, 6 January 2012, III, 7.

[10] *Roman Missal*, Second Sunday after Easter (or *of Divine Mercy*), Collect.

[11] Angelus, 25 March 2007.

[12] Homily, 15 May 2005.

[13] Homily, 29 September 2007.

[14] Homily, 13 April 2006.

[15] Address, 16 March 2007.

[16] Audience, 30 August 2006.

[17] Regina Caeli, 30 March 2008.

[18] Angelus, 8 February 2009.

[19] Angelus, 22 February 2009.

[20] Angelus, 15 February 2009.

[21] Angelus, 14 October 2007.

[22] Angelus, 31 October 2010.

[23] Angelus, 12 September 2010.

[24] Address, 7 March 2008.

[25] Homily, 11 May 2008.

[26] Regina Caeli, 12 June 2011.

[27] Regina Caeli, 11 April 2010.

[28] Audience, 19 October 2005.

[29] Audience, 7 January 2008.

[30] Homily, 15 May 2005.

[31] Homily, 5 February 2006.

[32] Audience, 5 May 2010.

[33] Homily, 15 April 2007.

[34] Homily [Sao Paolo, Brazil], 11 May 2007.

[35] Homily, 12 October 2008.

[36] Address [live broadcast via satellite, for the closing of the 49th International Eucharistic Congress, Quebec, Canada], 22 June 2008.

[37] Homily [World Youth Day, Cologne], 21 August 2005.

[38] Audience, 5 August 2009.

[39] Homily [Ecumenical Celebration of Vespers, Regensburg, Germany], 12 September 2006.

[40] Homily [Penitential Celebration with the Youth of Rome], 13 March 2008.

[41] Angelus, 16 September 2007.

[42] Address, 11 March 2010.

[43] Address, 25 March 2011.

[44] Address, 16 March 2007.

[45] Message, 12 March 2009.

[46] Address, 16 March 2007.

[47] Homily [Prison for Minors, Rome], 18 March 2007.

[48] Homily, 21 February 2007.

[49] Homily [Washington], 17 April 2008.

[50] Homily [Savona, Italy], 17 May 2008.

[51] Angelus, 15 February 2009.

[52] Audience, 27 February 2008.

[53] Audience, 19 October 2005.

[54] Homily [Canonization of Frei Antonio de Sant'Ana Galvao O.F.M., Sao Paolo, Brazil], 11 May 2007.

[55] Angelus, 8 December 2010.

[56] Angelus, 14 October 2007.

[57] Angelus, 19 August 2007.

[58] Angelus, 11 March 2007.

[59] Address, 16 March 2007.

[60] Angelus, 8 February 2009.

[61] Homily, 25 March 2007.

[62] Angelus, 25 January 2009.

[63] Homily, 20 March 2008.

[64] Homily, 7 March 2010.

[65] Homily [Ash Wednesday], 17 February 2010.

[66] Regina Caeli, 16 May 2010.

[67] Homily [Fatima], 12 May 2010.

[68] Angelus, 15 February 2009.

[69] Homily, 29 March 2007.

[70] Audience, 12 April 2006.

[71] Dialogue with the inmates of Rebbibia District Prison [Rome], 18 December 2011.

[72] Angelus, 21 March 2008.

[73] Homily, 29 March 2007.

[74] Address, 25 March 2011.

[75] Angelus, 22 February 2009.

[76] Audience, 19 October 2005.

[77] Address, 7 March 2008.

[78] Address [to the Roman Curia], 22 December 2011.

[79] Regina Caeli, 16 May 2010.

[80] Audience, 31 January 2007.

[81] Address, 7 March 2008.

[82] Catechetical Meeting with Children who had received First Communion during the Year, 15 October 2005.

[83] Letter to Seminarians, 18 October 2008, n. 3.

[84] Homily [Pastoral Visit to the Parish of 'God the Merciful Father', Rome], 26 March 2006.

[85] Homily [Serravalle, San Marino], 19 June 2011.

[86] Angelus, 31 October 2010.

[87] Homily [Prison for Minors, Rome], 18 March 2007.

[88] Angelus, 12 September 2010.

[89] Homily [Penitential Celebration with the Youth of Rome], 13 March 2008.

[90] Audience, 25 August 2010.

[91] Audience, 16 September 2009.

[92] Message, 12 March 2009.

[93] Address, 19 May 2011.

[94] Homily [Penitential Celebration with the Youth of Rome], 13 March 2008.

[95] Homily [Mestre, Italy], 8 May 2011.

[96] Homily, 29 March 2007.

[97] Homily, 15 April 2010.

[98] Audience, 21 February 2008.

[99] Angelus, 2 March 2008.

[100] Address, 7 March 2008.

[101] Homily [Penitential Celebration with the Youth of Rome], 13 March 2008.

[102] Audience, 1 July 2009.

[103] Homily, 11 May 2008.

[104] Homily [Aosta, Italy], 24 July 2009.

[105] Angelus [to English-speaking pilgrims], 22 February 2009.

[106] Angelus, 31 October 2010.

[107] Homily, 29 June 2009.

[108] Homily [New York], 19 April 2008.

The Gift of Faith

Insights for the Year of Faith
2012 - 2013

What is Faith? Where does it come from? Why does it matter? With Pope Benedict XVI's announcement of a Year of Faith, stretching from October 2012 to November 2013, these questions will be brought into sharp focus. In this simple yet profound booklet, Barbara Reed Mason uses the texts of the Second Vatican Council, the Catechism of the Catholic Church, the words of Pope Benedict XVI and Blessed John Paul II, as well as her own insights, to explore this vital area in a way accessible to every sincere searcher for truth.

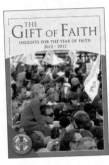

Barbara Reed Mason has been involved in faith formation for over twenty-five years, in the UK and internationally, giving retreats, talks and catechetical instruction to young people and adults.

ISBN: 978 1 86082 794 5

CTS Code: Do 856

Year of Faith with John Paul II

The Year of Faith will run from October 2012 to November 2013. One of the most public examples of faith in recent times was the late pope, Blessed John Paul II. This new booklet is a collection of encouraging speeches and addresses from this great disciple: from learning to love the Virgin Mary, to seeing joy as the "Keynote of the Christian message". His words serve as an indispensable guide for drawing closer to Christ and his Church.

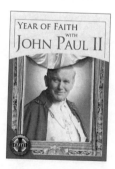

ISBN: 978 1 86082 793 8

CTS Code: Do 853

How to Spread the Gospel

Advice & Encouragement from Pope Benedict XVI

We are all called to spread our faith. In this virtual dialogue, an imaginary Catholic considers the challenges raised by evangelisation. The questions that he asks raise issues we might all encounter whilst trying to spread the Gospel successfully. The responses offered are taken from different instances of the preaching of Pope Benedict. This teaching is joyful and filled with hope, and makes evangelisation a service rather than a hardship, affirming everyone in their mission to be a fruitful apostle.

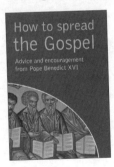

Fr Donncha Ó hAodha is a priest of the Opus Dei Prelature working in Dublin. Currently he works as chaplain to Rockbrook Park secondary school for boys and also to Nullamore Youth Centre.

ISBN: 978 1 86082 751 8

CTS Code: Do 847

Lumen

The Catholic Gift to Civilisation

In a recent debate, broadcast worldwide by the BBC, over 87% of the audience rejected the motion that the Catholic Church is a force for good in the world. To set the record straight, this booklet summarises the extraordinary fruitfulness of the faith, noting that our university system, art, music, legal tradition, charity and even much of our science arises from Catholic civilisation and Catholic minds. Besides encouraging Catholics, this booklet will be of great interest to teachers and general enquirers of some faith or none.

Fr Marcus Holden is parish priest of Ramsgate and Minster, Southwark, and course tutor and writer for the Maryvale Institute's M.A. in Apologetics.

Fr Andrew Pinsent is a priest of the diocese of Arundel and Brighton and Research Director of the Ian Ramsey Centre for Science and Religion at Oxford University. He was formerly a particle physicist at CERN.

ISBN: 978 1 86082 725 9

CTS Code: EV 6

Apologia

Catholic Answers to Today's Questions

The rise of secularism and the new atheists has led to many difficult questions being regularly posed about religion in general and the Catholic Faith in particular. This attractively illustrated booklet responds positively to questions about the existence of God, about science and faith, the Bible, the Church and the Sacraments and morality, setting out a reasoned defence of the truths of Faith that lead us all to greater happiness.

Fr Marcus Holden is parish priest of Ramsgate and Minster, Southwark, and course tutor and writer for the Maryvale Institute's M.A. in Apologetics.

Fr Andrew Pinsent is a priest of the diocese of Arundel and Brighton and Research Director of the Ian Ramsey Centre for Science and Religion at Oxford University. He was formerly a particle physicist at CERN.

ISBN: 978 1 86082 642 9

CTS Code: EV 5

Credo

The Catholic Faith Explained

This new, illustrated, pocket catechism offers a succinct and reliable introduction into the fullness of the Catholic faith. Drawing on Scripture and Tradition, and fully cross referenced to the Catechism and Compendium, its 25 chapters include:

The Meaning of Life
Creation & Fall
Salvation History
The Incarnation
The Life of Christ
The Paschal Mystery
The Trinity
The Church
Scripture & Tradition
Mary & the Last Things
Liturgy & Sacraments
Baptism & Confirmation
The Eucharist

Confession & Anointing
Marriage & Holy Orders
Moral Action
Natural Law & the Ten
    Commandments
Grace & the Beatitudes
Virtues & Vices
Christian Life in the world
The Life of Prayer
The Lord's Prayer
Praying the Mass
The Practice of Confession
Catholic Devotions

Fr Marcus Holden is parish priest of Ramsgate and Minster, Southwark, and course tutor and writer for the Maryvale Institute's M.A. in Apologetics.

Fr Andrew Pinsent is a priest of the diocese of Arundel and Brighton and Research Director of the Ian Ramsey Centre for Science and Religion at Oxford University. He was formerly a particle physicist at CERN.

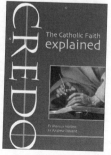

ISBN: 978 1 86082 470 8
CTS Code: EV 4